SUSTAIN

SUSTAIN

50 EASY TIPS FOR A CLEANER, GREENER, PLASTIC-FREE HOME

CHRISTINA STRUTT
of CABBAGES & ROSES

CICO BOOKS
LONDON NEW YORK

Published in 2020 by CICO Books
An imprint of Ryland Peters & Small Ltd

20–21 Jockey's Fields   341 E 116th St
London WC1R 4BW   New York, NY 10029

www.rylandpeters.com

10 9 8 7 6 5 4 3 2 1

A CIP catalog record for this book
is available from the Library of
Congress and
the British Library.

ISBN: 978-1-78249-833-9

Printed in China

Editors: Gillian Haslam
and Marion Paull
Designer: Elizabeth Healey
Photographer: Lucinda Symons

In-house editor: Anna Galkina
Art director: Sally Powell
Production manager:
Gordana Simakovic
Publishing manager:
Penny Craig
Publisher: Cindy Richards

Important note: always consult a
doctor or qualified herbalist before
treating any ailment using a herbal
remedy. While every attempt has
been made to ensure the information
in this book is entirely safe,
correct, and up-to-date at time of
publication, the Publishers accept
no responsibility for consequences
of the advice given herein.

Contents

Introduction

PLANET EARTH IS A RESILIENT PLACE: as humanity's canvas it has absorbed much and made way for so many of our inventions. Mankind is clever—too clever, perhaps. Our species has now entered its sixth millennia on the planet, and it is clear that for all our brilliance, wisdom has proved elusive—or is wilfully ignored. We cannot continue to think only of convenience and the immediate future. We need to change our ways to make sure that our beautiful planet can support us for many generations to come.

While scientists now talk openly about having passed the point of no return, they also assure us that if we mean business,

WE CAN MAKE A DIFFERENCE. Governments need to respond quickly and decisively—there must be no denial of the facts. But CHANGE STARTS AT HOME and, if we are united, the effect of such change could be dramatic. The nightly news may seem dismal, but there are chinks of light. I can see that the generation coming of age now really cares. They shall inherit this planet and they have no intention of being meek. I see community projects— the co-operatively kept hens that feed a neighborhood, the community gardens—and I see daily rounds of YouTube videos with ingenious ideas for repurposing the plastic we have consumed. I see the small businesses using compostable materials where plastics were once used, and I see a growing rejection of consumerism.

In this book *I hope to enlighten you on how to lead life in a more thoughtful, careful, organic, and ecologically friendly way.* Preparing your own cleaning products and growing your own organic fruit and vegetables is a safer, more environmentally sound way of living. It is possible to keep a clean house and maintain a fertile garden organically, to shop locally and seasonally, and to recycle and reuse as much as we possibly can. This way of life may sometimes be more time-consuming but, having tried and tested all the ideas in this book, I have found that it is more efficient and ultimately much simpler and less stressful.

Add to this the fact that you will save money, the environment, and miles traveled, and this can only be a good thing.

IF WE WERE TO ALL ADOPT THIS LIFESTYLE, IT WOULD HAVE A HUGE IMPACT ON OUR PLANET—that of being gentle with it. I have included only the tasks that I perform every year, every month, or every day in this book.

This is not a guide to sacrifice and hardship; on the contrary, it is a guide to embracing the gifts we have with great pleasure. If, in years to come, it is established that there was nothing we could have done to prevent climate change, the suggestions in this book can do no harm. If, however, in future we

9

see that together we all made a difference to prevent climate change and the disasters it might cause, then we can congratulate ourselves on a job well done. *We will be the beneficiaries of a world with a healthy population where fairness is the embodiment of ecological politics, and safety is at the heart of farming and manufacturing.*

THIS BOOK IS A VERY SIMPLE, pared-down version of all those many expert books on adopting a self-sufficient, organic lifestyle. It is for survival in a greener and more wholesome way. There is enough information to start you on your journey and to inspire you to do better, to be better, and to live a better life on a healthier planet.

THIS IS A RALLYING CRY TO ADOPT IDEAS FOR SUSTAINABLE LIVING, many of which tap into ancient ways and our collective consciousness. I hope that this book assists you in making those switches in every aspect of your domestic life. You have bought this book, and hopefully it will make a small difference in your life and a huge difference to the world as we know it.

Let us together do no harm.

CHAPTER ONE

Living mindfully

Cleaning

WITHOUT

chemicals

THIS IS BY NO MEANS a comprehensive list of how to keep your home clean. However, by using VERY FEW CLEANING PRODUCTS, you can achieve most household chores SIMPLY, EFFECTIVELY, NON-TOXICALLY, and SAFELY. This is a very simple, ordinary, day-to-day list of general housekeeping equipment, cleaning products, and techniques.

DISPOSABLE WIPES

THESE wipes ARE NOT
ENVIRONMENTALLY FRIENDLY.
Use them only in emergency situations.
The rest of the time, water and recycled
cloths will do the same job. If you have to
use a disposable wipe, *don't flush it away!*

NONTOXIC
Cleaning
products

THERE is a huge amount of organic and ECO-FRIENDLY CLEANING PRODUCTS available right now. However, many are very expensive and I find that the following basics are just as good. I have no need for anything more.

- Baking soda (bicarbonate of soda)
- Beeswax polish
- Borax substitute
- Distilled white vinegar
- Lemons
- Soda crystals
- PLUS: Feather or lambswool duster, rags, refillable spray bottles, and a range of brushes and brooms.

DISTILLED WHITE VINEGAR

FOR 10,000 YEARS this *fermented alcohol* has had hundreds of different uses. The Babylonians discovered its preserving properties; the Romans drank it; the Greeks pickled vegetables and meats in it; and soldiers during the American Civil War used it to treat scurvy. It heals wounds, cleans glass, and *melts away limescale and grease*. Once you realize how useful it is, you will probably want to stock up on industrial quantities of this magical liquid! Turn the page to discover some of its myriad uses.

THE
Magic *of* DISTILLED WHITE
vinegar

Altered hem and seam lines

IF YOU WANT to get rid of the holes created by taking down a hem or resewing a seam, iron the fabric over a cloth dampened with vinegar

Baby clothes

TO FRESHEN baby clothes, add 1 cup of vinegar to the detergent (washing powder) dispenser of the washing machine for the final rinse cycle. This will break down the uric acid and soapy residue on the clothes, leaving them soft and fresh. (You may also want to do this to liven up tired fabrics.)

Blankets

TO WASH wool or cotton blankets, add 2 cups of vinegar to the rinse cycle. This will make them soft, fluffy, and free of soap.

Boiled eggs

TO PREVENT an egg from leaking from its shell while it is being boiled, add a splash of vinegar to the water.

Burn marks

RUB neat vinegar onto the fabric with a soft cloth,

then rinse with water.
(Test on an inconspicuous
area first.)

Carpet stains

BLOT SPILLS as soon as
possible with a paper towel.
For a stain, mix 1 teaspoon
of dishwashing liquid
with 1 teaspoon of vinegar
dissolved in 2½ cups
(about 500ml) of lukewarm
water. Apply to the stain
with a soft cloth and rub
gently. Rinse with warm
water and blot dry.

Cooking odors

TO RID the kitchen of
cooking odors, simmer

a solution of vinegar
and water in a pan for
5 minutes.

Deodorant stains

TO REMOVE deodorant
stains on colored clothes,
rub with a soft cloth
dipped in vinegar and
wash as usual.

Drains

TO DEODORIZE drains,
pour a cup of vinegar down
the drain and leave for half
an hour, then flush through
with running cold water.
A mixture of vinegar and
baking soda will do the
job even more thoroughly.

Pour 2 tablespoons of baking soda down the sink hole followed by ½ cup of vinegar, leave to bubble for 20 minutes, then flush through by running the cold water for a minute.

Lime deposits in showerhead

IF THE SHOWERHEAD is clogged with lime deposits, soak in a bowl of one part vinegar to three parts water. Check after 30 minutes and rinse in cold water.

Lime deposits on faucets (taps)

SOAK A RAG in vinegar, then wrap it around the areas of buildup. Leave for 30 minutes, then rinse.

Microwave ovens

TO CLEAN and deodorize a microwave oven, fill a microwaveable bowl with vinegar, and boil in the oven. This will loosen dried food on the walls, which can then be wiped clean with a soft, damp cloth.

Painted walls and woodwork

MAKE a solution of two parts vinegar, one part baking soda, and three parts warm water. Dip a soft cloth into the solution and use it to wipe the dirt from the surfaces; rinse with clean water.

Red wine stains
BLOT THE STAIN immediately with a soft, dry cloth, and sponge with undiluted vinegar until it is gone.

Refrigerators
CLEAN the inside of the refrigerator with a solution made from equal parts of vinegar and water.

Sink garbage disposal units
TO CLEAN a sink garbage disposal unit, make ice cubes with one part vinegar and one part water. Put the cubes in the unit and switch on. This spatters the vinegar cubes throughout the system. Flush the unit with cold water afterward.

Steam irons
TO REMOVE lime deposits from steam irons, mix equal quantities of vinegar and distilled water, and fill the water chamber. Heat the iron for 5 minutes,

then press the steam button over scrap fabric to rid the chamber of the lime deposits. When cool, tip out the solution. Rinse the chamber well.

Toilet bowl staining
TO FRESHEN UP the toilet and remove stubborn stains, spray neat vinegar around the bowl and brush clean. Leave to soak overnight, if necessary.

Windows
MAKE a solution of one part vinegar and one part warm water. Pour into a spray bottle, then spray onto the glass. Rub the glass dry with a soft cloth, then polish with crumpled newspaper for a sheen.

Wooden chopping boards
VINEGAR or lemon juice will clean, deodorize, and disinfect wooden chopping boards. These are more hygienic than plastic ones.

MAGICAL *&* USEFUL CLEANING AGENT:

Baking soda

(bicarbonate of soda)

THIS IS ANOTHER MIRACLE of nature. Most baking soda is made from trona ore, which was discovered in the mid-1840s. Then, as now, it was used by many households for SCOURING, CLEANING, and DEODORIZING.

Brass

TO CLEAN brass, make a paste of baking soda and lemon juice. Apply and leave for a minute, then rinse well.

Carpets

SPRINKLE baking soda over carpets to deodorize them. Leave for an hour, then vacuum.

Chrome

FOR POLISHING chrome, make a paste of baking soda and water. Rinse thoroughly with clean water to remove deposits.

Dishcloths and washcloths (face flannels)

SOAK dishcloths and washcloths in a strong solution of baking soda and water to freshen them up.

Garbage cans (dustbins)

SPRINKLE baking soda into the bottom of garbage cans to remove unpleasant odors. After emptying the garbage, add some water and swill around the can. Pour the water out and leave the can to dry, then add more baking soda for next time.

Hairbrushes and combs

MAKE a solution of baking soda and warm water. Soak hairbrushes and combs for an hour to remove dirt and grease, then rinse with warm water.

Kitchens and bathrooms

WHEN MIXED with water, baking soda makes an alkaline solution that will cut through grease and dirt on most surfaces. Used dry, it is effective as an abrasive powder; mixed with distilled white vinegar, it becomes an even more powerful solution.

Mildew on shower curtains

TO REMOVE mildew growing on shower curtains, apply a paste of baking soda and water. Leave on the curtain overnight and wash off the next day with warm water.

Stains inside cups and teapots

FILL THE ITEMS with a solution of baking soda and water. Leave until the stain disappears, then rinse. For stubborn stains, use a solution of baking soda and distilled white vinegar.

Borax
SUBSTITUTE

AN EXTREMELY EFFECTIVE antibacterial and cleaning agent, borax substitute is almost as effective as commercial bleach. Make sure to wear protective gloves, as it is corrosive.

Carpet stains

MIX borax substitute with a little water into a paste. Test an area for color fastness, then rub into the stain, let dry, and vacuum off the powder. For wine stains, dissolve ½ cup of borax substitute in 2 cups of warm water. Rub into the stain, leave for 30 minutes, and sponge off.

Washing delicate items

SOAK in a solution of ½ cup of borax substitute with 1–2 tablespoons of detergent powder in a bowl of warm water. Rinse in cool water.

Lemons

A NATURAL DISINFECTANT AND STAIN REMOVER because of their acidity, cleaning with lemons will leave your home with a pleasant scent.

Countertop stains

SQUEEZE the juice of a lemon onto a countertop or cutting board to bleach stains. Leave until the stains disappear, then rinse.

Grout stains

MAKE a paste from lemon juice and a teaspoon of cream of tartar, and apply to the area with a toothbrush. Rinse with water.

Glass

MIX 4 tablespoons of lemon juice with 5 cups (about a liter) of water. Spray on glass and clean as usual.

Microwaves

PUT ½ lemon in a bowl of water and microwave for 45 seconds. Stains will be easier to clean and odors will be eliminated.

Beeswax

FOR CLEANING WOOD furniture, beeswax is infinitely preferable to the polish sold in aerosol cans, which contains silicone. Spray polishes create a shiny, impenetrable surface, whereas beeswax feeds the wood, giving it a luxurious, deep, well-fed shine.

It is not necessary to polish furniture more than about four or five times a year, provided it is kept dusted. (For intricately carved pieces of furniture or picture frames, a soft, fat, clean paintbrush can be used to remove dust from tricky corners.)

AN ALTERNATIVE TO BEESWAX is a DROP OF OLIVE OIL. This will feed the wood and, when buffed with a soft cloth, produce a lovely natural shine.

Kitchen
HYGIENE

I FEEL our dependence on antibacterial substances has made us a tad lazy in the kitchen-hygiene department. It is NOT NECESSARY TO RELY ON CHEMICALS to keep our kitchens clean and to avoid food poisoning.

- COOK your food thoroughly at high enough temperatures.
- WASH hands and surfaces thoroughly after handling raw meat.
- DRY your hands on a towel kept purely for that purpose, and do not be tempted to use the same towel to dry dishes.
- CHANGE dishcloths and dish towels (tea towels) every day. Keep them clean by boiling regularly in a solution of water and distilled white vinegar with a teaspoon of baking soda.

CHOPPING BOARDS

ALTHOUGH we were led to believe that plastic boards were safer than their wooden counterparts, research carried out by microbiologists at the University of Wisconsin's Food Research Institute in 1993 proved otherwise. Their study showed that germs placed on a wooden chopping board died within three minutes, but bacteria on a plastic board remained alive and multiplied overnight.

For this and many other reasons, it is always preferable to *use wooden rather than plastic chopping boards.* A sensible precaution is to keep boards used for bread and vegetables separate from those used for meat. To disinfect both wooden and plastic boards, spray with distilled white vinegar, leave for 30 minutes, then rinse.

HOW TO
stop using plastic food wrap

LIVING MINDFULLY

BEESWAX food wraps are an excellent alternative to plastic wrap (clingfilm), which contains the harmful chemical BPA (Bisphenol A). They are pieces of cotton that have been infused with beeswax, making them REUSABLE and BREATHABLE, as well as eco-friendly. When warmed by the hands, beeswax wraps become sticky, making it easy to cover bowls and wrap food such as sandwiches.

There are a multitude of options for alternative food covers, including glass, netting, wire, and fabric—SIMPLE MUSLIN is something often forgotten about. An upturned plate is great for covering food while it cools before going into the fridge. And don't forget about using good old-fashioned WAX PAPER—string or a rubber band will keep it in place.

Food
FRESHNESS

TODAY, an estimated ONE-THIRD OF ALL THE FOOD produced in the world GOES TO WASTE. That's equal to about 1.3 billion tons of fruits, vegetables, meat, dairy, seafood, and grains that either never leave the farm, get lost or spoiled during distribution, or are thrown away in hotels, grocery stores, restaurants, schools, or home kitchens.

- BY USING your sense of smell and your eyesight, and by buying from suppliers you trust, you will save a fortune by not throwing away food merely because packaging and "sell-by dates" tell you to do so.

- PLAN AHEAD and buy only what you need.

- USE YOUR FREEZER. While there are plenty of benefits to eating fresh food, frozen foods can be just as nutritious. Cooking and freezing food—especially produce—before it goes bad is a great way to avoid letting it go to waste.

- BE CREATIVE with leftovers. Before you shop, use the food you already have. Recipe websites allow you to search based on ingredients already in your kitchen.

Recycling
IN THE kitchen

AS MUCH AS YOU CAN, try to avoid buying food that has been excessively packaged. In recent years, many countries have introduced a charge on plastic bags, and some cities have banned them completely. You might think that paper bags are a more eco-friendly option, but their manufacture involves the destruction of huge areas of forest and the use of toxic chemicals.

The solution is to REUSE ANY BAGS you are given as many times as possible and, even better, to equip yourself with some permanent shopping bags, made of cloth or string. Keep some handy in your car or in your bag.

Local recycling schemes

In most cities, you can recycle glass, cans, foil, and plastic, and compost all cooked and uncooked food. I believe that if governments are truly concerned about recycling, they will make it simple for us to do. If this is not the case where you live, it is worth contacting your local government to ask why not.

COFFEE TO GO

A small but achievable aim is always to have a reusable cup with you for coffee or tea on the go, as coffee cups made of *paper and lined with plastic are non recyclable and go into landfill.*

CHAPTER TWO

THE
CONSIDERED
closet

DON'T BUY
"fast fashion"

BEFORE YOU BUY a new item of clothing, think about WHERE and HOW it has been made. It is becoming easier to source ORGANIC, or at least FAIR-TRADE, fabrics, and designers are more aware that the ethics surrounding the production of their garments are as important as their appearance. Increasingly, companies have a HIGHER LEVEL OF TRANSPARENCY, allowing you to see where their clothes are made, what materials they use, and how their workers are treated. Probably the best advice I can offer is:

- Be aware of social justice. That cheap T-shirt has an ethical price.
- Buy good-quality clothing for a fair price.
- Buy one good piece for every 10 cheap pieces you might have bought in the past, and look after it.

Wear
WHAT YOU'VE
got

One of the best ways of creating an ECO-
FRIENDLY WARDROBE is to buy as few new
clothes as possible. A good starting point is to
sort out your existing wardrobe and donate
what you haven't worn for over two years or
anything that no longer fits—this way you'll
inevitably REDISCOVER FAVORITES that
you might have forgotten about. Why not
organize a CLOTHES-SWAP party with
some friends; after all, one person's trash is
another's treasure!

THE ART OF REPAIR

When a hole or tear appears in a favorite item of clothing, *try patching it rather than throwing the garment out.* The patch should be of the same, or similar, material as that of the garment, but as for color and pattern—that all depends on what you can lay your hands on and your imagination. Try wonderful *Japanese sashiko* over the hole or patch for a beautiful finish. For other malfunctions, such as broken zippers, any good dry cleaner will have an invisible mending service.

Laundering
clothes

WASH COTTON and other machine-washable clothes at LOW TEMPERATURES with a cupful of baking soda (bicarbonate of soda) added to the detergent powder (washing powder). This makes the powder much more effective and helps to EXTEND THE LIFE OF YOUR WASHING MACHINE. Add a cup of distilled white vinegar to the dispenser drawer instead of fabric conditioner to remove chemical residues and soften the fibers of the clothes. Household linen, towels, and underwear can be washed at a temperature of 140°F (60°C) to destroy germs.

THE CONSIDERED CLOSET

When buying a new washing machine, check its green credentials and OPT FOR THE GREENEST APPLIANCE POSSIBLE—they are not necessarily more expensive. If you have the option of an ecowash in the program, use it.

TO TREAT STAINS, soak the item as soon as possible—fresh stains are much easier to deal with than dried stains—in a sink filled with a solution of baking soda and warm water. NEVER USE HOT WATER, as this can set the stain rather than remove it.

SMALL STEPS FOR
laundering clothes
THAT MAKE A big
difference

- INVESTIGATE "wet-clean" laundries to deal with your "dry-clean-only" items of clothing. They use a combination of steam, pure soap, and vacuuming to clean "dry-clean-only" clothes.

- INSTEAD of using bleach to whiten small cotton items, boil for a few minutes in a solution of water and lemon juice.

- HEATING the water accounts for 90 percent of the energy used in washing machines—the "warm" setting is warm enough.

- IF YOU want scented clothes and laundry, store lavender bags, soap, and essential oils in the linen drawer or closet. The linens will absorb the fragrances into their fibers.

🍃 USE POWDERED or tablet washing products in the washing machine and dishwasher. Liquid versions contain twice as many harmful chemicals.

🍃 AVOID using a laundry dryer (tumble dryer) as much as possible, not only to reduce carbon emissions but also to make your fabrics last longer.

IF YOU DISLIKE IRONING...

🍃 CLOTHES sold as "non-iron" are treated with formaldehyde, so avoid them.

🍃 CRUMPLED natural fabrics look better anyway.

Caring
FOR shoes

If you buy good-quality shoes, they should last for years with the following tips:

> ❧ Keep them clean and polished.
> ❧ Repair the soles and heels of shoes and boots as soon as possible to avoid permanent damage.
> ❧ Fill wet shoes and boots tightly with crumpled newspaper to keep them in shape, and leave them to dry naturally, then feed them with a really good natural polish.
> ❧ To remove odors from shoes, sprinkle baking soda (bicarbonate of soda) inside them and leave for a couple of hours.

CHAPTER THREE

Vintage
AND
preloved

Antiques fairs

HOW TERRIFIC would it be if, for just one season, everybody spent their time seeking out vintage clothes and furniture rather than new ones? Think of all the energy, pollution, and air miles that could be saved. Not only that, but older things are usually more beautifully made and they are more likely to be unique.

THIS QUOTE (opposite) by Edmond de Goncourt, an eminent French collector, in an old book written by Barbara Milo Ohrbach, sums up the rules...

" If you ever take up
collecting, each time you are
tempted by a work of art,
or by a curio, be sure to ask
yourself before deciding to
buy: can I live with it, keep it
in front of my eyes, and love
it until I die? **"**

Vintage
clothes

OLD TEXTILES ARE EXTRAORDINARY. The fact that something as simple as *a plain linen nightdress, woven by hand on a loom* and stitched together, may still be changing hands today is worthy of contemplation. Whether buying precious vintage items or simply preloved clothing from thrift stores, the following advice will help you to keep them at their best.

Cotton and linen

LUCKILY, cotton and linen are robust and sturdy fabrics, and respond well to washing. Most cotton and linen pieces can be gently handwashed, or washed in the machine on a gentle cycle. Never use hot water to wash delicate items. You must also NEVER USE CHLORINE BLEACH ON ANTIQUE FABRICS. Lemon juice will do just as good a job, but remember to rinse the fabric in warm water as soon as you have dissolved any stains.

Silk and embroidered fabrics

INTRICATELY embroidered pieces or fine silks might need expert advice before cleaning. Try to AVOID DRY-CLEANING—unless expressly advised—as the chemicals used may well do more harm than good. *Steaming is a good and gentle alternative*, although it is still worth taking advice before proceeding.

Drying delicate items

NEVER HANG delicate items to dry; always lay them flat on a cotton towel. Otherwise the weight of the water combined with gravity could well rip the fabric, especially if it is lace.

Storing textiles

WHEN STORING vintage clothing, it is best to lie garments flat and not hang them. If possible, roll rather than fold them as the fabric weakens along the folds.

MOTHS!

UNFORTUNATELY moths are a risk when you love vintage clothes, but they needn't be a problem if you are vigilant.

Before you introduce an item of vintage clothing into your closet, make sure to *wash it thoroughly* and dry it in bright sunshine. If the item is difficult or impossible to wash, *put it in the freezer* (in a bag or container to prevent condensation) for 48 hours.

Natural moth deterrents include:

- ❧ aromatic cedar chips
- ❧ bay leaves
- ❧ dried lemon peel
- ❧ lavender
- ❧ rosemary
- ❧ rose petals

OTHER PRECAUTIONS you can take are to *deep-clean your wardrobe* every few months and make sure all your clothes are clean before they go back in the wardrobe, as moths are attracted to unwashed clothes.

CHAPTER FOUR

Sustainable energy

FOR LIFE

Water

MANY PARTS of the world are experiencing dramatic, sometimes disastrous, extremes in their supply of water, Cape Town's recent drought and California's disastrous wildfires in 2018 and 2019 being just two examples among many.

EUROPE AND NORTH AMERICA still enjoy low-cost energy and an abundance of water, compared with many other parts of the world. As a result, we tend to squander these vital resources. We have huge reserves of cheap energy from prehistoric times, with vast areas of forest covering the land and enormous reserves of coal, oil, and gas, but all these gifts are finite, and all will eventually run out.

THE BAD PART about this dependence is the possibility that one day we may find ourselves without the fuel to warm ourselves, to transport food, and to run our factories. A solution to this and other impending self-inflicted problems is to WORK WITH THE NATURAL WORLD and DEVELOP OTHER SOURCES OF FUEL, so every country can be self-sufficient.

SUSTAINABLE ENERGY FOR LIFE

THE
cost *of* fuel

WITHOUT DOUBT, energy costs will—and should—rise. The cost of energy has to reflect not just the supply and demand issue, but also the environmental damage caused by different fuel sources. We are all in the same boat, because whichever country our unsustainable energy source comes from, the environmental impact is the same and affects us all.

ENERGY is a resource imported and exported throughout the world—often from areas of political instability—and with no guarantee that it will continue to be available at a price we can afford, at a time when we need it, from a country that is willing to sell it to us. EMERGING ECONOMIES ARE ENERGY-HUNGRY, and world reserves of hydrocarbon fuels are finite, with refining and distribution capacity struggling to meet demand—a demand that can only increase.

THE QUESTION we should ask ourselves is why continue the use of nonrenewable fuels when the damage they do to the environment is vast and their sustainability is in doubt. The *real change must come from government legislation* (such as signing the UN Paris Agreement) *and responsibility taken by large corporations.* According to the Carbon Majors Report of 2018, just 100 companies are responsible for 71 percent of global emissions.

63

Reducing OUR carbon footprint

WHILE THE MAJORITY OF CARBON EMISSIONS are not caused by individuals, there are many ways every one of us can LIMIT THE DAMAGE we are causing. The greatest energy consumption per person happens at home and during traveling. Both these areas are within our control to moderate.

Everyone will have their own financial and practical constraints, and *these measures may initially cost money, but in the long term they will be less expensive* than excessive oil or gas consumption, both to our pockets and, more importantly, to the environment. Here is a list of tips that are easy to follow and will make a difference:

- TRAVEL BY RAIL instead of by air when possible, and consider offsetting the carbon footprint of your journey.

- DRIVE LESS—try walking or cycling whenever possible.

- THINK ABOUT buying an electric or hybrid car if you cannot use public transportation; they are decreasing in price every year.

- DON'T BUY FAST FASHION—see *The Considered Closet* (pages 40–41) for how to kick this habit.

- WEAR MORE CLOTHES when it is cold, rather than switching on or turning up the heating.

- **LIMIT YOUR USE** of air-conditioning in the summer by using electric fans, or create a through draft by opening doors and windows that are opposite each other.

- **GET YOUR HOUSE** inspected by a qualified insulation advisor. You will receive advice on all aspects of energy saving, not to mention money saving.

- **IF WINTERS ARE COLD** where you live, you should be aware that properly insulated wooden floors absorb heat and keep it for longer than vinyl or tiled floors.

- **FOR EXTRA PROTECTION** from cold drafts, consider having your drapes interlined with felt.

SUSTAINABLE ENERGY FOR LIFE

- **PLACE A BRICK** or a filled bottle of water inside the toilet tank. This will save at least 1 quart (1 liter) of water for every flush.

- **BRUSH YOUR TEETH** with the faucet (tap) turned off (an obvious one, but still something many people forget).

- **ONLY BUY** appliances that are certified as energy-efficient.

- **STOP EATING** (or eat less) meat. Just limiting your meat consumption can make a huge difference. To produce a single pound of beef, it takes over 5,000 gallons (22,730 liters) of water—as the number one consumer of freshwater in the world, animal agriculture is increasing the problem of water scarcity.

RUN THE DISHWASHER or washing machine with full loads.

KEEP APPLIANCES running efficiently so that they use less electricity. Keep the heat exchanger at the back of the refrigerator dust-free, and regularly clean the inside of the dishwasher and washing machine with a solution of distilled white vinegar and baking soda.

DEFROST your freezer regularly and fill the empty parts of the freezer with bags of ice.

SWITCH OFF unnecessary lights and use localized lamps instead of overhead lighting.

USE LOW-ENERGY light bulbs. By changing all your normal light bulbs to compact fluorescent bulbs, you could save

75 percent of the energy you would have used.

ა UNPLUG ALL electronics when they are not in use, as when they are switched off but left plugged in, they are still draining energy.

ა BOIL ONLY as much water as you need.

ა CHOP VEGETABLES SMALLER so that they cook more quickly, using less power.

ა

Alternative
ENERGY SOURCES

ONCE WE HAVE REDUCED OUR ENERGY demand, we need to look at how to generate our reduced energy needs from fuels and sources that do not damage the environment. These should be sustainable and available locally, where possible, to give us the security of supply.

FOR MANY, especially those who live in urban areas, the options for alternative fuels and energy sources for homes are more limited than for those who live in semi-rural and rural areas, purely because of space. *However, there are systems tailor-made for individual properties and community schemes that are kind to the environment.* Check the websites of energy providers to discover whether you are in a position to receive greener power.

Wind farms and wind turbines

The capital cost of setting up wind farms is huge because the infrastructure required to connect them to the electric grid is costly. However, they work only when the wind blows, so we cannot yet depend on them entirely. That being said, THE UNITED KINGDOM IS THE WINDIEST PLACE IN EUROPE with enough offshore wind to power the country three times over. In the United States, where wind power varies greatly from region to region, the picture is more complex, but technology enabling the networking of individual sites to equalize overall production is improving, and larger, more efficient turbines are being built.

FOR INDIVIDUALS, the options are to buy energy from a "green" supplier, or, subject to planning regulations, to install your own wind turbine (and solar panels). If you live in a very windy part of the world, the local utility will buy your wind power if you have a surplus.

SUSTAINABLE ENERGY FOR LIFE

Solar power

EITHER DIRECT SOLAR HEAT OR PHOTOVOLTAIC CELLS GENERATE ELECTRICITY. The technology is getting better and less costly, and can work well for individual houses.

LOCAL GOVERNMENT CAN HELP BY REVISING PLANNING CODES to make them less restrictive for the installation of solar panels, and designers can help by improving their appearance. As part of a multi-technology installation, solar power can contribute all year round.

Tidal power and hydropower

ALTHOUGH NOT A VERY CONVENIENT SOLUTION FOR inland populations, tidal power is another option. The tide is guaranteed, and the power systems using tidal power are known to work. However, the capital costs are enormous. Hydropower has proved itself to be efficient, albeit with huge installation costs, and requires ugly pylons and cables. While the infrastructure could be buried underground, environmental damage might outweigh the benefits. However, it is another option for the experts to work on. Individual homes or communities can benefit from hydropower if there is access to a water resource of sufficient volume and flow.

Biofuels

THESE FUELS are produced from material that has been grown specifically for fuel production, or from material grown for other purposes that has generated a by-product once called "waste." This is a knee-jerk, selfish, and not very efficient policy to create road fuel. Worse still is the ripping up of rainforest to accommodate palm oil plantations. THESE PRACTICES ARE COUNTERPRODUCTIVE AND ECOLOGICALLY DISASTROUS.

THE future
of energy supply

WE CAN ALL HELP SIMPLY BY REDUCING OUR DEPENDENCE ON CARS. If you can't get by without one, consider buying an electric or hybrid car. Governments can help by making public transportation more user-friendly, cheaper, and more efficient, and we can all do our part by using it. Even though apps like Uber and Lyft are convenient, they contribute to an increase in city traffic and a decrease in demand for public transportation.

SUSTAINABLE ENERGY FOR LIFE

TO BEGIN WITH, we need to focus on converting existing agricultural and forestry by-products and waste to a fuel source that can be utilized to produce heat and, to a lesser extent, power. This can range from wood chips to straw and cereal wastes and processed wood waste. *There is also the option of converting animal and human waste to generate electricity and heat.* Incineration of domestic and industrial waste—subject to careful control of incineration flue gases—is also a viable concept at an industrial scale, as well as on a smaller scale.

SUSTAINABLE ENERGY FOR LIFE

Forestry benefits

INCREASING THE AREA OF LAND UNDER FORESTRY to produce sustainable wood for fuel would provide an endless resource. Planting and managing woodland also reduces carbon emissions because of the carbon dioxide absorbed and the oxygen given out by growing trees, and land is also stabilized by tree roots. This would vastly improve the biodiversity of woodland, create employment in rural areas, and provide a source of income for woodland owners. More than 5.5 million tons (5 million tonnes) of wood waste is committed to landfill every year in the United Kingdom alone. In the United States, the figure is about 29 million tons (26 million tonnes).

SUSTAINABLE ENERGY FOR LIFE

WOOD WASTE can be recycled in other ways besides fuel (for example, as wood chips for mulch), but its use as fuel is arguably the most important. Wood produces neglible amounts of sulfur—the substitution of wood for bituminous coal reduces sulfur emissions by 80 percent. And emissions of carbon dioxide are about 1 percent of those for burning oil. INDUSTRY IS BEGINNING TO REALIZE THE ECONOMIC VALUE OF THIS FORM OF RECYCLING. In the Southeast and Pacific Northwest of the US, wood-related industries are supplying more than half of the energy they need by burning wood waste.

Nuclear energy

IN THE UNITED KINGDOM, which lacks the vast forest reserves of North America, nuclear fuel is advocated by some people as a "clean" option. However, a typical nuclear power plant generates about 22 tons (20 tonnes) of used nuclear fuel per year which is HIGHLY RADIOACTIVE AND POTENTIALLY DANGEROUS. It has to be carefully handled and stored (which costs a lot of money), and it requires a large amount of specially designed storage space.

SPENT NUCLEAR FUEL takes hundreds of years to decompose before it reaches adequate levels of safety. This issue, combined with the relatively few but still catastrophic nuclear accidents that have occurred, are problems that other energy sources simply don't have to deal with.

CHAPTER FIVE

A USEFUL
garden

Local
AND SEASONAL

THE PERFECT WAY to cut down your food miles is to grow your own fruit and vegetables. Eaten moments after picking, they taste so much better than those transported halfway around the world. If you're lucky enough to have a backyard, what you can grow is limited only by your climate and imagination, while urban dwellers without much outdoor space can grow fruit and herbs in window boxes and containers.

Garden compost

COMPOSTING EASES THE LOAD OF WASTE collectors and therefore the quantity of landfill waste. If you have outdoor space, *consider starting a compost bin*. There is something magical in the way that waste products become a valuable source of nutrients and improvers for the soil, giving back what has been taken from it.

THE JOY OF COMPOSTING

- Garden compost enriches the soil by increasing the organic matter, so that plants are healthier.

- Compost provides slow-release nutrients.

- Not only does compost help the soil to retain moisture, it also balances the pH levels.

- Compost reduces soil erosion.

- In winter, the compost increases soil temperature, while in the summer it lowers it, thus benefiting the plants.

- Sandy soils improve by gaining body, which will preserve moisture, and clay soils will gain a more open structure, so they drain better.

Local government composting schemes

MANY CITIES now have their own food-waste collection schemes. If you do not have the space for your own compost bin, this is an easy way to send less food to landfill.

40 percent of household waste can be composted at home, saving 20 percent of the UK's methane emissions from the slow decomposition of biodegradable landfill waste.

THE COMPOSTING ASSOCIATION

Community gardens

IF YOU DON'T HAVE A BACKYARD, see if there is a community garden in your area. Where I live in the UK, the standard community garden is what we call an allotment garden, some of which have been in use for more than 150 years.

IN OTHER PLACES, too, the value of community gardens is increasingly being recognized. Recent decades in the United States have seen a steady rise in their number —communal gardens occupy formerly vacant lots in downtown areas, and these gardens play a major role in fostering a strong community spirit.

INFORMATION ON COMMUNITY GARDENS (in Canada and the United States), as well as guidelines for starting and running them, can be obtained from the American Community Gardens Association (www.communitygarden.org).

Growing
YOUR OWN

GROWING FROM SEED IS THE SIMPLEST
and least expensive method of raising large
numbers of plants. All you need to know will
be on the seed packet, unless you have been
given seeds by a grower, in which case ask
them for the sowing instructions. As a general
rule of thumb, seeds should be sown at a
depth equal to their thickness.

TENDER PLANTS that will be affected by frost should be started in a cold frame or indoors in a greenhouse in late winter/early spring. In mid-spring, sow hardy annuals directly into the ground where you want them to grow and flower. Herbaceous plants can be sown indoors in late winter or outdoors in late spring. Once you have made your planting plan and bought your seeds, there is nothing to stop you from starting to grow your own flowers and vegetables for the season ahead and, if stored carefully, into the winter, too.

Materials and equipment

POTTING COMPOST Make sure this is organic. *Never buy peat, as this is an unsustainable product* which, even though organic, is not ecologically friendly. Use a good commercial potting compost mixture designed for seedlings, with a loose, crumbly texture, consisting mainly of sterilized loam and sand.

SEED TRAYS OR SMALL POTS An egg tray is a very eco-friendly container for small seedlings, allowing them to be planted directly into the soil in their own little biodegradable pots without disturbing the tiny root systems. *If you are reusing an old seed tray or pot, make sure it is clean and does not carry old viruses or molds* from previous plantings or old age. To disinfect them, wash with a solution of one part warm water and one part distilled white vinegar.

Which crops to grow from seed

I SUGGEST YOU EXPERIMENT—you will soon find out what suits your soil, your climate, and your patience. *To avoid gluts of the same foods, sow as wide a variety as possible,* and try to plant crops that can be harvested at different times of the year. It is also wise to choose those vegetables and fruits that are expensive to buy, as well as, of course, the ones that you are particularly fond of.

Flowers

THE THREE SPECIES of flowers that I grow abundantly in my garden are roses, sweet peas, and lavender. These are generous in their provision of cut flowers, simple to grow, and undemanding in their need for attention. As with most of what is available to buy, it is better by far to *support local growers and nurseries*—partly because the indigenous species they grow will thrive, but mainly because they are a dying breed; as long as there are huge nurseries cornering the market, supplying cheap but ordinary plants, their livelihoods and expert knowledge are in danger of disappearing.

A USEFUL GARDEN

A SEASONAL GUIDE TO
growing
your own
PRODUCE

THIS SEASONAL LIST will help you plan your garden month by month. In addition to helpful advice on vegetables, there is information on growing fruits and flowers.

Spring

🌰 KEEP DIGGING to prepare the soil, applying garden compost and manure, and a good sprinkling of Epsom salts (see pages 115–117).

🌰 START successional sowings of salad crops.

🌰 COVER emerging shoots with muslin or burlap (hessian) when there is danger of frost.

🌰 SORT OUT your seeds into months for sowing.

🌰 SOW FAVA BEANS (broad beans) outside— the earlier they are sown, the hardier they will be. They will also be less prone to attack by blackfly.

🌰 PLANT carrot and any other seeds suitable for early sowing, following instructions on the packets.

- DIVIDE plants to increase your stock and make more space.

- ORGANIZE plant swaps with friends and neighbors.

- WHERE NECESSARY, support plants with bamboo sticks firmly pushed into the ground. Do this before the plants start toppling over, so that you are less likely to damage roots when inserting the sticks and can encourage plant growth in the right direction from the start.

- REGULARLY hoe between rows to keep the soil free of weeds.

- EARTH UP POTATOES to encourage a good crop.

Summer

ം CONTINUE successional sowings of flowers and vegetables.

ം PLANT OUT tender vegetables and ornamental plants as soon as all risk of frost has passed.

ം PLAN TIME OFF, so you can make use of your crops when they are ready to be frozen or made into pies, jellies, ferments, and relishes.

ം REGULARLY DEADHEAD roses to encourage further flowering.

ം WATCH OUT for aphids, blackfly, and other pests. On strong, healthy plants, use a hose to wash them off or wipe them away with a gloved hand.

ം IN LATE SUMMER, harvest crops such as onions and shallots, leaving them to dry in the sun.

- CUT HERBS and dry or freeze them to use throughout the winter.

- DIG UP perennial weeds, such as dandelions and docks, completely removing the roots from the soil.

- AT FIRST sight of bindweed, dig gently down to its root, remove carefully, and destroy.

Never put bindweed in the compost bin—put it on a bonfire.

- SPRAYING neat vinegar onto weeds growing in difficult-to-access places will get rid of them permanently.

- REMEMBER to stop and savor the beauty of your garden.

COMPANION PLANTING

ENCOURAGE PREDATORS, such as ladybugs and hoverflies (*syrphid flies*), by companion planting. This involves growing pollen-rich flowering plants close to vegetable plants to attract beneficial insects. *Marigolds smell bad to aphids and attract hoverflies, which feed on aphids.* Companion plants can also be used to entice destructive pests away from crops. For example, nasturtiums are easy to grow from seed and are a popular companion plant for cabbages and lettuces because they attract caterpillars.

Fall

- **PICK AND STORE** vegetables before the first frosts arrive.

- **TIDY** fallen leaves and other debris, collecting sticks and pine cones for use as fire lighters.

- **CONTINUE** with the harvest, preserving and freezing your produce.

- **PLANT** winter salad crops in pots to grow on the windowsill.

- **CHECK** your apples kept in storage, and immediately remove any that are showing signs of deterioration.

Winter

ON FINE, mild days, begin digging the border and the vegetable patch.

CHECK stored vegetables and fruit, and remove any that are not healthy.

PROTECT tender plants with muslin or burlap (hessian) covers.

Prune fruit trees and roses.

PLANT bare-rooted shrubs and trees.

SEND for seed catalogs and plan your planting for the new year ahead.

YOU CAN CONTINUE to harvest winter crops such as rutabagas (swedes), parsnips, brussels sprouts, leeks, and cabbages.

KEEP turning your compost heap.

IF YOU have bought a Christmas tree growing in a pot, it's a good idea to repot it into a larger pot and feed it, then leave it outside until next Christmas.

CLEAN TOOLS and wipe them down with a rag dipped in olive oil.

SHARPEN cutting tools and then wipe them with an olive-oil rag.

Rain

BEFORE THE ONSET OF "DECKING MANIA," heavy rain was accommodated by lawns and flower beds. Now the water just runs off into drains, and heavy downpours, combined with thousands of decked gardens, result in huge quantities of water overwhelming the drainage systems. LESSON NUMBER ONE: *Reinstate your lawn and your flower beds to slow down the water runoff.*

FLOWER BEDS might seem like hard work compared to pots, but, on the whole, looking after a small flower bed is less work than looking after pots. For one thing, when it does rain, there are deeper reserves in the soil than there are in pots, and there is also so much more choice when planting a flower bed. From flowers for cutting to vegetables and fruit, there is so much more scope to be self-sufficient with a flower bed.

COLLECTING RAINWATER

DEPENDING ON WHERE YOU LIVE—and whether or not mosquitoes, which are attracted to standing water, are a serious problem in your area—you may be able to *store rainwater in a barrel or storage tank*. But first check your local building codes to make sure this is legally permissible. If it is, make sure to position the tank away from areas where you eat or sunbathe.

HOWEVER, there are more decorative options, such as a garden pool or even a little waterfall or fountain (the small pumps required use little electricity). Any flies or mosquitoes should be kept in check by dragonflies, while with clever planting around a pool, you can encourage predators, such as frogs, to take up residence.

Making the most of water

It is important to water plants efficiently, and there is much that can be done to preserve and protect plants during periods of drought. Make sure your soil's structure is as good as it can be, with adequate additions of organic matter to all soils, and sand to heavy clay soils. *Install a water barrel or storage tank to collect rainwater* (if permissible in your area), and make sure your gutters are clear of leaves and other debris for good flow.

- Mulch plants with a good layer of wood or bark chips, which conserves moisture and also suppresses weeds.

- Keep flower beds free from weeds, which compete with your plants for nutrients and water reserves.

- Water with a watering can, and pour the water directly onto the roots. Don't overfill the can, making it heavy to carry, because the water is easily spilt.

- Always water during the early morning or in the evening, when your efforts won't be wasted by the drying effects of the sun.

- Choose plants that are suited to your environment—it makes life so much less complicated.

- Bathwater and dishwashing water that do not contain any toxic chemicals can be used to water plants. This method of watering is best kept for flowering plants, rather than food plants.

- In containers, use water-retaining granules, which conserve water and release it slowly.

Feeding plants
—THE MAGIC OF
Epsom salts

ALONG WITH HOMEMADE ORGANIC garden compost, a major, but little-known, asset to the gardener's store cupboard is a good supply of Epsom salts. The benefits of this completely natural compound to the garden are numerous—I cannot recommend Epsom salts highly enough.

STUDIES HAVE SHOWN that magnesium and sulfur (two of the components of Epsom salts) enrich the soil to benefit vegetable crops and flowering plants.

The benefits of using Epsom salts include:

- Helping seeds to germinate.
- Promoting bushier plant growth.
- Encouraging plants to produce more flowers, leaves, and fruit.
- Increasing chlorophyll production in plants.
- Improving the phosphorus and nitrogen uptake of plants.

APPLY THE SALTS EVERY 4–6 weeks throughout the growing season from spring until early fall. Dissolve four handfuls into 2½ gallons (about 10 liters) of water—this quantity will drench a 50-square-foot (about 5 square meters) plot. Alternatively, sprinkle around the roots of plants and water in. When planting new rose trees and bushes, sprinkle a handful into the newly dug hole before planting. Apart from garden compost and manure, *the only substance I use to encourage growth in my garden is Epsom salts.*

CROP ROTATION

TO KEEP SOIL HEALTHY, crop rotation is an essential part of organic gardening. This is because each crop tends to leach the soil of a particular nutrient. *Crop rotation allows the nutrient balance to become re-established*, and prevents pests and diseases particular to specific crops from building up in the soil. Never plant the same crop in the same bed for two years running. Keep planting plans from year to year, because it is very easy to forget which plant has been grown in which bed.

GARDEN
pests

THE BATTLE AGAINST PESTS in the garden is never-ending, which makes it very tempting to resort to toxic chemicals. However, as well as being unkind—I hate the thought of even a slug dying a slow and painful death—toxic substances are not necessary, because there are other methods that are just as effective.

Natural pest control

All the natural methods of pest control that follow here are as adequate as their chemical counterparts. Unlike commercial pesticides, they do not harm the natural predators of pests, or the environment. One of the

117

most effective ways to prevent infestation is to establish strong, healthy plants. In my experience, these are better able to survive an occasional attack from small pests if you are vigilant and react quickly.

Slugs and snails

MAKE HUMANE TRAPS for slugs and snails by burying bowls of beer in the soil, pouring in enough beer to drown a decent-sized slug. The enticing odor of the beer will attract the pests so that they slither into the bowl, get drunk, and drown. Milk is an alternative lure, but I prefer the idea of a drunk slug drowning to the rather sweet idea of a slug with milk whiskers. *Remember to empty the traps often and renew the beer;* this is not a pleasant task but is infinitely preferable to the disappointment of watching all your hard work in the garden disappear in a slime trail.

ENCOURAGE WILDLIFE, such as birds and frogs, which will feast on slugs. *Whatever you do, don't use lethal slug pellets, as these are also lethal to the slugs' and snails' natural predators.* Harmless garden snakes, such as garter and milk snakes, should be allowed to go about their business—which includes preying on your resident gastropods. Learn to identify these useful reptiles and make them welcome.

Gardening
FOR wildlife

Bees—the gardener's friend

It is thought that there are 30,000 different species of bees in the world, and one-third of our food supplies depends on pollination by bees and other insects. Encourage bees to visit your garden by planting blue, white, yellow, and purple flowers for their ultraviolet properties.

Ladybugs

Encourage ladybugs into your garden because they eat aphids such as blackfly. Ladybugs like to lay their eggs in nettles, so leaving a small nettle patch to flourish in your garden should increase ladybug numbers. One ladybug that lives for one year can eat more than 5,000 aphids. If a plant is infested with aphids, don't panic and spray it with a chemical pesticide—once ladybugs reach that plant, they will eat the aphids quickly.

SHRUBS FOR WELCOMING WILDLIFE

Butterfly bush (*Buddleia davidii*)

English ivy (*Hedera helix*)

Escallonia

Heather (*Calluna vulgaris*)

Firethorn (*Pyracantha*)

White hebe (*Hebe albicans*)

Lavender (*Lavandula*)

Lilac (*Syringa x hyacinthiflora*)

Waxyleaf privet (*Ligustrum quihoui*)

Blackberry (*Rubus fruticosus*)

Sage (*Salvia officinalis*)

Thyme (*Thymus vulgaris*)

CHAPTER SIX

Cooking
AND
eating

Shopping
RESPONSIBLY

MUCH OF WHAT WE BUY *from a grocery store has traveled an average of 12,500 miles (20,000 kilometers).* Whether we are growing food ourselves or not, it would be an enormous contribution to lessening the effects of global warming if we were, as much as we possibly can, to shop locally, seasonally, and organically.

Local producers

I HAVE TO ADMIT that I often find myself in a grocery store. I am not suggesting that grocery stores are an expendable commodity—they clearly have a place in our time-restricted lives. However, more consideration should be taken as to where they are located, the way they treat their suppliers, and the damage they do to the business of smaller, local stores. I believe *the resurgence of specialist food stores and farmers' markets is proving we do understand that eating seasonal, locally produced food is an important factor in reducing our carbon footprint.*

Seasonal food

THE TIME HAS COME for us to realize the great impact of having nonseasonal produce in our stores, and of imported food replacing what we can grow easily on our own doorstep. To wait for the local strawberry season is not a hardship. We should and must ask ourselves whether a bowl of strawberries flown in from hundreds of miles away is a necessary extravagance.

TAKE HOME LESS PLASTIC

GROCERY-STORE PACKAGING *is responsible for 4.6 million tons of waste generated every year in the UK* alone. It is us who buy and dispose of the packaging, and it is therefore up to us to stop buying such overpackaged produce. Produce bought at farmers' markets is usually placed right in your shopping basket or bag.

THE TRADITIONAL
pantry

TO MAKE USE OF SEASONAL FOODS without daily trips to the grocery store, a good pantry is essential. This can be just an area of the kitchen or the utility room, fitted with lots of shelves and concealed with one or more doors. If you're lucky enough to have a separate room to use as a pantry, I recommend keeping it cool, so that you can use it to prechill cooked dishes and as temporary cool storage over the holidays, when the fridge is full to bursting.

Pantry ingredients

For rainy days and hungry guests:

- ❧ Dried beans—chickpeas, flageolets, navy (haricot), kidney
- ❧ Dried fruit—apricots, figs, raisins, etc.
- ❧ Jars of homemade jams, jellies, chutneys, pickles, ferments, and other relishes
- ❧ Organic flour
- ❧ Organic oats—for cooking, baking, and bathing
- ❧ Organic pasta—a good selection of sizes and shapes
- ❧ Organic tomatoes—canned or bottled

Produce to grow in large quantities because it stores well:

- Apples
- Beets (beetroot)
- Garlic
- Nuts
- Onions and shallots
- Potatoes
- Small fruits
- Tomatoes—to use fresh, in chutneys, or in sauces

Food items to buy when you don't know what to choose:

- Lemons—for a million reasons
- Organic butter
- Organic eggs
- Organic milk and cream

Harvesting
AND storing

THE MOST IMPORTANT RULE in the storing of produce, whether bought or grown yourself, is to store only perfect fruits and vegetables. When harvesting, *separate any damaged fruit or vegetables and use immediately*; dispose of anything that looks infected on a bonfire.

PERFECT SPECIMENS are less likely to deteriorate in storage and more likely to keep for months. Pick vegetables at their optimum size—the younger, the better—over a period of time. The aim is to avoid finding yourself picking old, stringy vegetables or gigantic peas, because the effort involved in preserving them will be somewhat wasted.

REMEMBER that the more young, succulent vegetables you pick, the more the plant will respond by producing more.

A WELL-STOCKED FREEZER

ONE OF THE FEW modern-day inventions that can make up for its carbon footprint in usefulness is the freezer. Well stocked and efficiently run, it can save many a trip to the grocery store. It is also invaluable for storing seasonal fruit and vegetables from the garden or from the market, to keep you fed throughout the winter months.

Preserves, jams, jellies, pickles, ferments, and drinks

WHEN YOU FIND yourself with a glut of fruit and want to preserve some of your crop, or when produce is in season and therefore cheaper, make some jam or pickle it. *Fermenting and pickling is a tradition that has had a recent surge in popularity, and is well worth trying out for yourself.*

HOMEMADE PRESERVES also make a lovely gift. However, when you look lovingly at the "fruits" of your labor, it can be quite hard to give them away. A gift of homemade jam is so precious that you might become quite mean-spirited and need to think hard about whether the recipient is deserving enough! A clever way around this is to make sure to keep a stock of small preserve jars—particularly sweet are

132

the miniature versions of the "Le Parfait" spring-lidded jars. It is far easier to part with a little jar than a whopping great one!

TO MAKE up for that rather cruel and selfish last paragraph, may I suggest that a generous gift would be to present a selection of jams packed in a box.

The secret of making preserves is to follow the recipes in minute detail, measure the fruit and sugar carefully, and follow the timings precisely. There is a wealth of recipes online and many dedicated preserving bibles that you can buy or borrow for inspiration.

THE
usefulness
of herbs

SINCE THE life-changing discovery of antibiotics, we have grown to expect quick solutions to our health problems. *It is estimated that of the 83 million prescriptions issued annually in the United States, outside hospitals, for antibiotics alone, some 50 million are unnecessary.* Comparable figures apply in the United Kingdom.

Medicinal herbs

USED TO TREAT various ailments since the beginning of time, herbs and flowers are the basis for many modern-day pharmaceutical drugs. Like our ancestors, we discover their benefits by trial and error in scientific research. Two medicinal plants that spring to mind are *the yew tree, the toxic berries of which are a vital part of tamoxifen, an estrogen inhibitor used in the treatment or prevention of cancer*, and the evening primrose flower, which has many applications in hormonal medicine.

Ancient remedies

DURING EARLY MEDIEVAL TIMES, the word "herb" denoted all useful plants, which included vegetables as well as herbs as we know them today. It was not until the eighteenth century that herbs were given their own category, distinguishing their medicinal and life-enhancing properties from those of food plants. Alongside vegetable gardens, infirmary gardens were cultivated to grow specific herbs for the apothecary.

BE SAFE

HERBAL MEDICINES can be as powerful as their chemical counterparts prescribed by doctors, so it is absolutely vital that before treating any ailment you SEEK THE ADVICE OF A QUALIFIED HERBAL PRACTITIONER. Synergism—which is the effect created by combining more than one herbal remedy— can enhance the effect or can make it extremely dangerous. This is another reason why you should always get advice.

Other than as flavoring in cooking, *herbs should never be taken during pregnancy or by children under five years old.*

Protecting wild herbs

INTEREST IN HERBAL MEDICINE IS INCREASING. The more knowledgeable and informed we become about the side effects of conventional medicine, the more we seek alternative remedies—homeopathic, floral, and herbal. This renewed interest has a downside, though. It was always believed that herbs gathered from the wild were more efficacious than cultivated plants, and *90 percent of all herbs used in medicine today are still gathered from the wild.*

ACCORDING TO THE VEGAN SOCIETY, the herb goldenseal (*Hydrastis canadensis*), used for immune deficiency problems, is now listed by CITES (Convention of Trade in Endangered Species) as the fifth most endangered plant species on the planet. *When buying herbal tinctures and preparations, check that all ingredients come from sustainable sources*, and that a registered, ecologically sound company manufactures the product.

Growing herbs

THE BEST OPTION is to grow your own herbs and, with the advice and help of your practitioner, make your own remedies. If you find that a specific herb eases symptoms or guards against your particular weaknesses, make sure to have your own sustainable supply. Herbs make beautiful and useful growing companions for flowers, fruit, and vegetables. *Their strong scents can not only act as deterrents to pests, but also encourage those creatures most likely to feed on any that do persist.*

Popular medicinal herbs

THE FOLLOWING LIST includes herbs that are commonly grown or easily found. *I stress again that, unless you are using herbs to flavor food and drinks, you should seek advice from a herbal practitioner.* Never rely solely on home treatment for any medical complaint.

ALLHEAL (*Prunella vulgaris*), also known as self-heal, woundwort, or sticklewort, grows wild throughout temperate regions of the world and is easy to establish. Allheal is useful for treating sore throats and inflammations of the mouth.

ALOE VERA'S healing powers are very *effective in the treatment of sunburn and other minor burns.* The gel extruded when the leaves are cut can be applied to all sorts of wounds. It forms a protective layer and encourages skin regeneration.

CHAMOMILE (*Matricaria chamomilla*) is commonly used for its sedative properties, but it also relieves morning sickness, hemorrhoids, mastitis, eczema, and hay fever.

CLOVES (*Syzgium aromaticum*) have extraordinary healing and pain-relieving powers, and medicinally no other substance has been found to equal their efficacy in relieving toothache.

COMFREY (*Symphytum officinale*) is mainly used in poultices to heal wounds and reduce bruising. Its leaves contain allantoin, an agent that stimulates healthy tissue formation, which probably explains why it is often used in the manufacture of skin-softening cosmetics.

DANDELION (*Taraxacum officinale*) has many uses, and all of the plant is safe to use. The young leaves, collected before the flowers appear, are good in salads, contain more iron and calcium than spinach, and are rich in vitamins A and C. The leaves are a powerful diuretic, and can be boiled with honey to treat coughs.

FENNEL (*Foeniculum vulgare*) leaves, seeds, and the bulb can all be used. Fennel seeds steeped in water make a remedy for digestion, heartburn, and constipation.

LAVENDER (*Lavandula angustifolia*) oil made from the leaves has a beneficial effect on stings, burns, cuts, and grazes. Adding the oil to a warm bath helps to relieve headaches and ensure a good night's sleep.

LICORICE (*Glycyrrhiza glabra*) has been used medicinally for over 3,000 years. The dried root, which is stripped of its bitter outer bark, is used as a remedy for colds, sore throats, and bronchial catarrh.

MARIGOLD (*Calendula officinalis*) is known for its antiseptic, antifungal, and antibacterial properties and is used in the preparation of calendula cream—a homeopathic remedy effective in treating burns, grazes, scalds, and stings.

PARSLEY (*Petroselinum crispum*) is rich in vitamin C, minerals, and the antiseptic chlorophyll. It can help in relieving urinary infections and, in poultices, acts as an antiseptic dressing for wounds, sprains, and insect bites.

ROSEMARY (*Rosmarinus officinalis*) is steeped in myth and magical tales. Rosemary oil is a very powerful agent, and must be used with care and never taken internally. Its antibacterial properties make it a good addition to bathwater for healthy skin.

SAGE (*Salvia officinalis*) can be used to treat colds and, when made into a tisane with a little cider vinegar, is effective as a gargle to treat sore throat, laryngitis, and tonsillitis.

HERB TEAS

BOTH MEDICINALLY AND FOR PURE PLEASURE, fresh or dried herbs make a gentle and refreshing alternative to normal tea. Mix with fresh orange or lemon peel for added flavor, and sweeten with honey, if desired. *Use 1 teaspoon for each cup of boiling water, and leave to steep for 5 minutes.* The following herbs all make delicious teas: Basil, caraway, chamomile, fennel, fenugreek, hibiscus, lavender (use both the leaves and the flowers), lemon balm, lemon verbena, mint, rose petal, rosemary, sage, and thyme.

CHAPTER SEVEN

Natural beauty

Glow
FROM WITHIN

IN THE LAST FEW YEARS, THE BEAUTY INDUSTRY
has undergone a revolution as customers have demanded
greater transparency. It is now simple to find out exactly
what's in every product you put on your body. With organic
ingredients, vegan beauty, and cruelty-free all becoming
buzzwords, it has never been easier to choose products that
not only work well, but are also made in a more sustainable
way. *One of the best ways of avoiding plastic packaging
and unnecessary ingredients is to make your own simple
preparations at home.*

HOMEMADE
beauty
preparations

Basic body scrub

SMOOTH, blemish-free skin is easily achieved with the help of just a few basic ingredients. You can be sure that homemade scrubs are pure, and they can be custom made to suit all types of skin.

1 cup (225g) coarse sea salt
4 tablespoons olive oil
Juice of 1 lemon or lime

MIX all the ingredients together and rub all over the body once a week to exfoliate the skin, concentrating on problem areas, such as knees, feet, and elbows; then shower off. The lemon or lime juice in the mixture acts as a bleaching agent, which will whiten your finger- and toenails.

Bath salts

TO MAKE bath salts, fill jars with natural coarse salt and add either olive oil or a scented oil. Lavender oil makes very beautiful bath salts and will promote restful sleep. Other herbs, oils, and fresh or dried flowers can be added—try rosemary oil with a sprig of rosemary, or rose oil with dried rosebuds. If using fresh herbs or flowers, use within one or two weeks, before the flower petals or leaves lose their color.

Refreshing morning bath tonic

FOR an extremely invigorating tonic, add crushed wormwood leaves to cider vinegar and let infuse. Store in a glass jar with a nonmetallic lid.

ADD this to running bathwater in the morning for a fresh start to the day.

Bath teas

INFUSE fresh bay leaves in boiling water and add the strained bay tea to a hot bath to relieve aching limbs. For healthy skin, pour a cup of rosemary tea into bathwater.

Marshmallow hand lotion

THIS is a wonderful lotion for dry, chapped hands.

½ cup (28g) marshmallow
  root
Cold spring water
2 tablespoons ground
  almonds
1 teaspoon milk
1 teaspoon cider vinegar
Lavender or olive oil

CHOP the marshmallow root finely and soak in cold spring water for 24 hours. Stir and strain well through a cheesecloth-lined sieve. Add 1 tablespoon of the marshmallow juice to the ground almonds, milk, and cider vinegar. Mix together with a few drops of lavender oil if you want a scented lotion; use olive oil if you do not. Pour into a clean, dry, screw-top jar and keep in the fridge, using as required.

Strawberry face pack

THE JUICE and flesh of fresh strawberries make a lovely face pack, exfoliating the skin and lightening dark spots. Mash the fruit and spread all over the face—lying down so that it doesn't slide off. After 20 minutes, wash off the face pack.

Epsom salts

EPSOM SALTS ARE VERY USEFUL IN THE GARDEN (see pages 115–117). However, they have many beauty uses, too. They contain magnesium sulfate, which is absorbed through the skin when added to bathwater. This draws toxins from the body, soothes the nervous system, reduces swelling, relaxes tired muscles, is a natural emollient, and an excellent exfoliator.

NOTE: *It is important to check with your doctor before using Epsom salts if you have any health concerns.*

Bath soak

ADD 2 cups of Epsom salts to your bathwater to enjoy a relaxing and sleep-inducing bath.

Skin exfoliator

MASSAGE handfuls of Epsom salts over wet skin in the shower, starting with your feet and continuing up toward the face. Rinse off with warm water.

Foot soak

TO SOOTHE aches, remove odors, and soften rough skin, add ½ cup of Epsom salts to a large bowl of warm water. Soak your feet for as long as you like, then rinse in warm water and dry thoroughly.

Sprains and bruises

EPSOM SALTS will reduce the swelling caused by sprains and bruises. Add 2 cups to a warm bath and soak.

PLASTIC-FREE PERIODS

SANITARY PRODUCTS ARE THE FIFTH MOST common item found on Europe's beaches, more widespread than single-use coffee cups, cutlery, or plastic straws. *It is estimated that 700,000 panty liners, 2.5 million tampons, and 1.4 million sanitary towels are flushed down the toilet every day in the UK.*

ALTERNATIVES ARE STARTING TO CATCH ON: There are tampons with reusable applicators, as well as tampons made of organic cotton. Another option that has become popular is the silicone menstrual cup, which recoups its cost after about four months of use compared to single-use methods.

Finally...

IF YOU HAVE READ THIS BOOK FROM COVER TO COVER, I hope it will have made an impact on the way you live day to day. If ecological issues become so much a part of all our lives, we will begin to take for granted that lights are never left on unnecessarily; that we never throw things away which can be recycled or re-used; that we never leave water running unnecessarily.

If we refuse to accept plastic bags and excessive packaging, then without noticing we will be making a huge difference. If we just stop, take stock of the way we live, and do 10 of the things listed here every day for the rest of our lives, then we will make a difference. If we can stop climate change in its tracks, then we can feel less ashamed when we hand our beautiful planet over to the next generation.

- Switch off all unnecessary lights
- Shower for one minute less every day
- Grow three herbs
- Walk instead of using the car once a week
- Take a vacation at home now and then
- Plant grass instead of installing decking
- Recycle all your paper
- Try using the cleaning products listed in this book for one month
- Do not buy single-use plastic bottles or cups
- Place a brick in your toilet cistern
- Make your next car a hybrid or electric model
- Buy local and seasonal food when you can
- Turn your heating down, and wear more clothes when it gets cold
- Buy a fan so you can use less air-conditioning
- Take the train instead of an airplane
- Take a bicycle instead of the car
- Walk to your destination once a week
- Learn to respect the planet
- Teach your children to respect the planet

Useful contacts

ENERGY

www.ases.org
The American Solar Energy Society provides
information on solar energy.

www.eere.energy.gov/greenpower
Energy Efficiency and Renewable Energy,
a US government site—advice on finding
a green energy supplier.

Good Energy
www.goodenergy.co.uk
A British company supplying only
100-percent renewable energy.

HOME AND GARDEN

Cabbages & Roses
www.cabbagesandroses.com
A family-owned fashion and fabric company.
Made as much as possible with www.oekotex.com
standards, in limited quantities, in the UK.

Colour Makes People Happy
www.makespeoplehappy.co.uk
An entirely natural, eco-friendly paint company.

Dalefoot Composts
www.dalefootcomposts.co.uk
Suppliers of peat-free and bracken-based potting mix.

Edward Bulmer Natural Paints
www.edwardbulmerpaint.co.uk
Nontoxic natural paints made from raw materials such
as plant extracts, chalk, earth minerals, and linseed.

Little Greene Paint & Paper
www.littlegreene.com
Odorless, water-based paints with the industry's lowest
eco-rating and with virtually zero Volatile Organic
Compounds (VOCs).

BEAUTY AND FASHION

AS Apothecary
www.asapoth.com
A small-batch distillery making natural scents,
creams, aromatic waters, and balms.

Beyond Skin
www.beyond-skin.com
Ethically made vegan footwear.

Depop
www.depop.com
Buy and sell fashion online.

Vestiaire Collective
www.vestiairecollective.com
Platform for selling unwanted designer clothes
and accessories.

FOOD

http://afsic.nal.usda.gov
The Alternative Farming Systems Information
Center, a US Department of Agriculture body,
offers a wealth of information on sustainable
food production.

www.ams.usda.gov/farmersmarkets/map.htm
How to find farmers' markets in your state.

Riverford Organic Farmers
www.riverford.co.uk
Organic fruit and vegetables from a cooperatively
run farm.

www.wholefoodsmarkets.com
Leading retailer of natural and organic foods.

GENERAL

Ebay
www.ebay.com

Real Simple
www.realsimple.com
A treasure trove of inspiring ideas for the home.

Sustainable Food Trust
www.sustainablefoodtrust.org
Working to accelerate the transition to more
sustainable food and farming systems.

Index

ACKNOWLEDGMENTS To all those who are making us aware of our beautiful, beautiful planet and are working toward solutions to save it.